BIRDS IN ECUADOR

A Photographic Journey

Glenn Bartley

Conservation in Ecuador

Mindo Clouforest Foundation (MCF) is an Ecuadorian non-profit conservation group with members from 5 countries. We specialize in linking birding tourism to habitat conservation. In addition to various community based conservation initiatives, MCF owns and operates two popular bird sanctuaries in the Andean foothills and tropical lowlands - Milpe and Río Silanche respectively. We also pioneered the creation of the Paseo del Quinde – South America's first Eco-scenic route/birders´ trail.

Our bird sanctuaries are part of an altitudinal transect linking the Tropical Andes and Tumbes-Chocó-Magdalena biodiversity Hotspots as characterized by Conservation International, and are in or near three Birdlife International designated Important Bird Areas (IBAs) in Northwestern Ecuador. Our lands and activities help protect an important suite of avian species—including 70 regional endemic, 11 vulnerable and 2 endangered species - along with many boreal migrants and species categorized as Near Threatened.

In Ecuador there has been a lot of political change since Sept, 2007. A new constitution mentions the rights of the "Paccha Mama" (mother earth in Quichua) and, at least on paper, calls for the defense of the country's biodiversity. The current government has even initiated some promising programs, e.g. Socio Bosque (Forest Partners) to pay select landowners $30 a hectare per year to maintain native forests. At the same time, the government is especially determined to initiate major mining activities. MCF is meeting the challenge of confronting these shortsighted endeavors by creating incentives that connect habitat conservation with the improvement of local living standards.

We believe that an active civil society with members that include conservation organizations helps create meaningful dialogue about important issues that can either destroy habitats or help build them. At MCF we are helping create new economic incentives for ecologically amenable land use. This is the biggest challenge to bird conservation in Ecuador and throughout the world.

The foundation commemorated seven years of operations in December, 2008, and updates regarding foundation activities are available for download on our website - www.mindocloudforest.org

When MCF president Brian Krohnke met Glenn Bartley at a conference in Texas in 2008, he knew there was a cool opportunity for collaboration. We love Glenn's work and think it shows some of the best of the Ecuadorian avifauna. Part of the purchase price of this book will help support our efforts. Thank you!

President, Brian Krohnke - info@mindocloudforest.org

The East
The Sierra
The West
The South

THE EAST

▲ A Yellow-tufted Woodpecker forages for food high atop a massive Ceibo tree.

► Trogons, such as this male Amazonian White-tailed Trogon, often perch motionless for long periods of time – scanning the forest for insects to feed on.

▲ A pair of White-fronted Nunbirds.
▼ The impressive bill of this White-eared Jacamar is used for snatching butterflies and other insects from the air.

▲ The canopy-dwelling Pied Puffbird.

▼ The fruit of the Cecropia tree is a favourite for many species of birds – including this White-throated Toucan.

▲ The diet of parrots consists mainly of fruit. To aid in digestion however, parrots such as these Cobalt-winged Parakeets must visit clay licks on a daily basis.

◀ Ivory-billed Aracaris roam the Amazon in large groups as they search for food.

▼ A Dusky-headed Parakeet feeds on clay alongside the Napo River.

▲ A female Amazon Kingfisher calling to its mate.
◄◄ The Ringed Kingfisher is the largest of the 6 species of New World Kingfishers.
▼ This male Green Kingfisher proudly displays his freshly caught Piranha.

▲ The tiny American Pygmy Kingfisher searches for prey amongst the flooded trees.
▼ Green-and-Rufous Kingfishers are elusive residents of shady Amazon streams.

▲ Easily identified by their bright yellow head and white eye – the male Golden-headed Manakin is an inconspicuous resident of Amazonian Ecuador.

◀ The Red-capped Cardinal is a flashy bird that is generally easy to see along streams in the Amazon.

▲ A Black-capped Danocobius calls from an exposed streamside branch.
◀ Striated herons are common in the lowlands on both sides of the Andes.
▼ The prehistoric looking Hoatzin is a unique resident of flooded forests and the only member of the monotypic family Opisthocomidae.
►► The Crested Owl (p.20) and Tawny-bellied Screech Owl (p.21) in the Amazon.

▲ The long and slender toes of the Purple Galinule help it to walk across aquatic vegetation.

► White-winged Swallows are often found feeding on insects above bodies of water in the east.

▼ The normally shy Sungrebe emerges from cover to cross a stream.

▲ Torrent Ducks live in fast moving rivers and streams on both slopes of the Andes.
◀ A Chestnut-crowned Antpitta in the forest understorey.
▼ The female Torrent Duck is as attractive as her mate.

▲ The Golden-tailed Sapphire can often be found at forest edges or clearings in the eastern foothills.
▼ Fork-tailed Woodnymphs are largely forest-dwelling species but will occasionally come out to the edges to feed.

▲ As opposed to the white boots found in the western race, Booted Racket-tail hummingbirds found in eastern Ecuador have buff coloured boots.

►► The Sword-billed Hummingbird (p.28) has proportionately the longest bill of any bird in the world. A Black-throated Brilliant in the eastern foothills. (p.29).

▼ A Gray-chinned Hermit feeds at a Heliconia flower.

▲ The bumblebee like male White-bellied Woodstar feeds at a flower.
◀ The Chestnut-breasted Coronet is an aggressive species found generally above 2000m on both slopes.
▼ A male Long-tailed Sylph proudly displays his shimmering tail.

THE SIERRA

▲ A Carunculated Caracara perched in paramo grassland.

◄ The endemic Ecuadorian Hillstar lives on high arid slopes where it feeds primarily on the orange flowers of the Chuquiragua shrub.

►► A Rufous-bellied Seedsnipe in its high elevation habitat.

▼ The Black-faced Ibis is now found only near the Antisana and Cotopaxi volcanoes.

▲ A male Tit-like Dacnis high upon the El Cajas plateau near Cuenca.
► Unlike most members of the Grallaria family, the Tawny Antpitta is easy to see in its preferred habitat above 3000m.
▼ Tufted Tit-Tyrants are common in shrubby areas of the highlands on both slopes – including Quito's Parque Metropolitano.

▲ A White-chinned Thistletail perches briefly atop a branch while gleaning insects from the highland vegetation.

◄◄ A Black Flowerpiercer perched atop a flower (p.40). Viridian Metaltails are found almost exclusively at forest borders on the east slope (p.41).

► A Shining Sunbeam pauses momentarily on a dead branch – taking time to stretch its wings.

▲ Cinerous Conebills are often seen as they actively glean insects from the undersides of leaves.

► The male Black-tailed Trainbearer proudly displays his impressive tail – the longest of any Ecuadorian Hummingbird.

◄◄ An Ash-breasted Sierra-Finch singing from a lichen-covered branch at the Jerusalem forest preserve (p.44). Often difficult to get a clean look at, the Azara's Spinetail is a notorious skulker (p.45).

►► Blue-mantled Thornbills are one of the few species of hummingbirds that will actually land on the ground to feed (p.48). The Sapphire-vented Puffleg is a stunning resident of the highlands throughout the Ecuadorian Andes (p.49).

▲ High in the dry open paramo habitat the Paramo Ground-Tyrant perches on a lichen-covered rock.

◀ A Red-rumped Bush Tyrant in the Cajas National Recreation Area.

▼ A Giant Conebill is typically found in paramo forest habitats where it searches for insects underneath the paper-like bark of the Polylepis trees.

▲ A Plumbeous Sierra-Finch surrounded by the unique vegetation of the paramo.
► The common and conspicuous Great Thrush.
▼ One of the most common birds of Ecuador's paramo zone is the Bar-winged Cinclodes.

▲ An Andean Coot emerges from the reeds of one of Ecuador's high altitude lakes.
▼ An Andean Gull in a flooded grassland.

▲ Ecuador's highland areas are home to most of the country's duck species. Here a pair of Andean Teals stroll through the wet grasslands.

►► The Great Saphirewing (p.56) and Tyrian Metaltail (p.57) are two of the wonderful hummingbirds that can be found at the Yanacocha reserve.

▼ The male Andean Ruddy Duck is easily identified by its bright blue bill.

THE WEST

▲ During spring migration along the coast a Wandering Tattler forages for food to fuel its long journey north.
► The Black-necked Stilt shows off its ultra-long Legs.
▼ A Collared Plover basks in late afternoon sunlight.

▲ The Blue-footed Booby is certainly one of Ecuador's most famous birds. Normally associated with the Galapagos Islands – this individual was photographed much closer to the mainland near Isla de la Plata.

▼ A Nazca Booby keeps its mouth open to try to cool down as it sits in the hot coastal sun on Isla de la Plata.

▲ A female Magnificent Frigatebird perched near its nesting colony.
►► A male Green-crowned Brilliant approaches to land on a Heliconia flower.
▼ A Brown Pelican gracefully soars above the ocean near Puerto Lopez.

▲ A Lesser Nighthawk roosts on a fallen tree.

◀ A Gray Hawk calls for its mate in a coastal forest near the Ayampe River.

▶▶ A pair of Masked Trogons – the female (p.69) is eating a large moth.

▲ The Immaculate Antbird searches the forest floor for insects.
◀ The incredibly shy Giant Antpitta pauses momentarily on a moss covered stump before hopping back into the dense undergrowth.
▼ Deep in the forest Andean Cock-of-the-rocks gather at "lek" sites where they call and display for females.

▲ The Tropical Parula warbler is a common bird throughout the west.
► A White-whiskered Puffbird in the humid lowland forests.
◄◄ A Western Emerald hummingbird feeds at a forest flower.
▼ Rufous-tailed Hummingbirds are found exclusively in the west.

▲ A Pale-mandibled Aracari displays his impressive bill.
◀ One of Ecuador's most spectacular hummingbirds – the male Violet-tailed Sylph.
▼ A Flame-faced Tanager feeds on a fruiting tree near Mindo.

▲ Tanagers seem to come in every colour of the rainbow. Here a Golden-naped Tanager poses on a mossy branch.

◄◄ A Montane Woodcreeper (p.78) and Crimson-mantled Woodpecker (p.79).

▼ The Black-chinned Mountain-Tanager is often found in monotypic flocks of up to ten individuals.

▲ A Black-capped Tanager is a bird that is uncommonly found in the northwest.
▼ The Golden Tanager is one of Ecuador's most common canopy dwellers.

▲ The female Booted Racket-tail lacks the ornamental tail feathers and boots of its mate.

◀ The tail of the male Booted Racket-tail hummingbird has to be seen to be believed.

▲ It is easy to understand how the Purple-bibbed Whitetip hummingbird earned its name.

▼ A White-whiskered Hermit extends its bill deep into a flower to feed.

▲ The colour of hummingbirds is due to iridescence – where certain wave lengths of light are absorbed and others reflected. Depending upon the angle upon which it is viewed, the Velvet-purple Coronet can look black or a dazzling shade of purple.

►► A Buff-tailed Coronet feeds at a flower in the forest understorey.

▲ Euphonias can be a difficult family of birds to tell apart. Here a male Orange-bellied Euphonia shows off the gorgeous contrast between blue and gold.
► An Andean Emerald takes a momentary rest on a mossy branch.
▼ The charismatic Toucan Barbet is found only on northwest Andean slopes.

▲ This chubby Barred Becard often accompanies mixed species flocks.

◀ A Spotted Woodcreeper works its way up a dead tree searching for insect prey.

▶▶ Spotted Barbtails (p.92) and Moustached Antpittas (p.93) are shy denizens of the forest understorey.

THE SOUTH

▲ A stunning White-necked Jacobin hummingbird feeds at a flower.
◀ The brilliant gorget colours of the Amethyst-throated Sunangel light up the cloudforest.
▶▶ A Violet-bellied Hummingbird perches on a Heliconia flower.

▲ In the southeast of Ecuador tanager diversity can be mind boggling. Each of the four photographs presented here were taken from the same Cecropia tree as a mixed species tanager flock passed through. Above a Bay-headed Tanager perches on a Cecropia leaf stem.

▼ A Green and Gold Tanager also takes part in the feast.

▲ A Golden-eared Tanager waits for its turn to feed at the ripe fruit.
▼ A Blue-necked Tanager enjoys a mouthful of a Cecropia catkin.

▲ A Masked Flowerpiercer looms near a hummingbird feeder – waiting for an opportunity to steal some of the hummingbird's nectar.

◀ The Jocotoco Antpitta is a critically endangered species that was only discovered in 1997.

▲ A Rainbow Starfrontlet approaches to feed at a flower. This species is most easily seen in Ecuador at the Utuana reserve.

◀ Of all the hummingbirds it is the sunangels that seem to have the most vibrant gorgets. Here a Purple-throated Sunangel perches on a lichen covered branch.

▶▶ The odd looking male Wire-crested Thorntail (p.106) alongside a Coppery-chested Jacamar (p.107).

▲ A Magpie Tanager perches atop a tree to oversee its surroundings.
◀ Smooth-billed Anis are usually found in large groups in grasslands and disturbed habitats.
▶▶ An Emerald-bellied Woodnymph feeds at a bromeliad flower.

▲ A Lacrimrose Mountain-Tanager works its way through the treetops searching for food.

◀ A handsome Rufous Antpitta hops about in the forest undergrowth searching for a meal.

▼ A Bananaquit poses on a mossy branch.

▲ The brilliant yellow Saffron Finch lives only in the south where it can often be found in small flocks.

◀ A Brown Violetear perches on a branch displaying its lovely violet ears.

▼ Largely frugivorous, Green Honeycreepers will also feed on nectar at humming bird feeders.

▲ A small group of Pacific Parrotlets perched on a thorny shrub.
◀ The common and widespread Rufous-collared Sparrow sings from an exposed perch.
▼ A Tropical Gnatcatcher sings from a branch in the dry arid scrub of south Loja.

▲ Yellow-browed Sparrows are common in grassy areas where they are often spotted foraging on the ground.

► It is hard to imagine how a bird could be more colourful or representative of tropical birdlife, than the gaudy Paradise Tanager.

www.glennbartley.com